Look What Came From Africa

by
Miles Harvey

Franklin Watts

A Division of Scholastic Inc.

New York Toronto London Auckland Sydney

Mexico City New Delhi Hong Kong

Danbury, Connecticut

Series Concept: Shari Joffe
Design: Steve Marton

Content Consultant: Myra Gordon, Ph.D, Associate Dean
for Diversity and Curriculum, College of Arts and
Sciences, Virginia Polytechnic Institute and State University

Library of Congress Cataloging-in-Publication Data

Harvey, Miles.
   Look what came from Africa / by Miles Harvey.
      p. cm. — (Look what came from series)
   Includes bibliographical references and index.
   Summary: Describes many things that originally came from
Africa, including music, dance, foods, animals, fashion, and art.
   ISBN 0-531-12050-3 (lib. bdg.)   0-531-16626-0 (pbk.)
      1. Africa--Civilization—Juvenile literature. [1. Africa—
Civilization. 2. Civilization, Modern—African influences.]
I. Title. II. Series.

DT14 .H35 2001

960—dc21

                                              2001046795

Photographs © 2002: America's Shrine to Music Museum, University of South Dakota, Vermillion, SD: 9 left; Archive Photos/Getty Images/Scott Harrison: 7 top left; Art Resource, NY: borders 4-32 (The Newark Museum), 22 right (Manu Sassoonian), cover top, 23 bottom left (Werner Forman Archive/Ghana National Museum); Bridgeman Art Library International Ltd., London/New York/Josef Herman Collection, London: 22 left; Corbis Images: 7 bottom left (Bettmann), 1, 8 inset (Cathy Crawford), 9 right (Owen Franken), 13 bottom left (Philip Gould), 21 left (Kelly-Mooney Photography), 7 top right (Julie Lemberger), 13 top right; Envision: 12 top right, 13 top left (Peter Johansky), 13 top center (Steven Needham); Lauré Communications: back cover; Nance S. Trueworthy: 26 left, 26 right; National Geographic Image Collection/John W. Vandercook: 8; National Museum of African Art, Smithsonian Institution: 25 bottom right (Franko Khoury/Acquisition grant from the James Smithson Society, 89-8-2), 19 center (Franko Khoury/Gift of Philip L. Ravenhill and Judith Timyan, 91-3-5), 25 top right (Franko Khoury/Museum purchase, 91-14-1); Peter Arnold Inc.: 15 left (Fred Bruemmer), 12 bottom left (David Cavagnaro), 32 left (Gerard Lacz), 14, 15 far left (Thomas D. Mangelsen); Photo Researchers, NY: 15 bottom right, 17 left (Nigel J. Dennis), 17 top right (Renee Lynn), 11 bottom left (Charles D. Winters), 16 left (Art Wolfe); PhotoEdit/Phil Borden: 9; Rigoberto Quinteros: 19 right, 19 left; Stock Boston: 23 right (Michael A. Dwyer), 10 right, 11 top left (John Elk III), 3, 20 left (Owen Franken), 12 top left and center (John Lei), 21 bottom right (Lawrence Migdale), 18 left (Frank Siteman); Stone/Getty Images: cover background (Tim Davis), 7 right (Hulton Getty), 15 top right (Nicholas Parfitt), 16 right (Art Wolfe); The Image Works: 18 right (Bill Bachmann), 17 bottom right (Tom Brakefield), 20 right (Richard Lord), 6 (Joe Sohm), 10 center (Topham); TRIP Photo Library: 7 bottom right (R. Belbin), 10 left (TH-Foto Werbung); Victor Englebert: 24 right, 24 left, 25 left; Viesti Collection, Inc./TRIP: 13 bottom right; Visuals Unlimited/Inga Spence: 11 right; Wolfgang Kaehler: 23 center; Woodfin Camp & Associates: cover bottom (M & E Bernheim), 21 top right (Christy Gavitt), 27 (Betty Press).

Map on page 5 by Lisa Jordan

Contents

The Cradle of Civilization

If you look at a world map, you can't miss Africa. It is the second-largest continent on Earth. In fact, Africa takes up one-fifth of all the land in the world. It includes fifty-four different countries and is made up of many, many ethnic groups.

Scientists have evidence that modern human beings originated in Africa between 100,000 and 200,000 years ago. These early human beings are ancestors of all the people in the world today. In other words, we all come from Africa! Also, Africa was the site of some of the world's oldest civilizations. That's why Africa is known as the "cradle of civilization."

About 500 years ago, a terrible thing happened to Africans that will forever link them to the Americas. Europeans began kidnapping Africans and sending them to their colonies to work as slaves. Between the 1500s and the 1800s, millions of Africans were thrown into chains, shipped across the Atlantic Ocean, and forced to work their entire lives without pay.

But even though the Africans did not choose to leave their homeland, they brought with them many things that have enriched American culture. Much of the music we listen to, the food we eat, and the art we love had their beginnings in Africa. So come on! Let's check out some of the amazing things from Africa!

ATLANTIC OCEAN

ASIA

INDIAN OCEAN

Banjo

Morocco
TUNISIA
ALGERIA
LIBYA
EGYPT

MAURITANIA
SENEGAL
GAMBIA →
GUINEA BISSAU →
GUINEA
MALI
BURKINA FASO
NIGER
CHAD
SUDAN
NILE
ERITREA
DJIBOUTI

SIERRA LEONE
IVORY COAST
GHANA
TOGO
BENIN
NIGERIA
CENTRAL AFRICAN REPUBLIC
ETHIOPIA
SOMALIA

LIBERIA

COFFEE

EQUATORIAL GUINEA →
CAMEROON
GABON
CONGO
DEMOCRATIC REPUBLIC CONGO
UGANDA
RWANDA →
BURUNDI →
KENYA
TANZANIA

CORNROWS

GIRAFFE

ANGOLA
ZAMBIA
MALAWI
MOZAMBIQUE
MADAGASCAR

NAMIBIA
ZIMBABWE
BOTSWANA
SWAZILAND
SOUTH AFRICA
LESOTHO

tap dancing

N

Music and Dance

One of the most wonderful things that Africans brought to the Americas was their incredible love of music and dance. In fact, many types of modern American music—including **gospel, blues,** and **jazz**—have their roots in traditional African music. Also, did you know that **hip-hop** and **rhythm and blues** are constructed from traditional African rhythms and forms?

In Africa, music and dance were inseparable. So it's not surprising that elements of African dance forms also made

Gospel choir

Blues musician
B. B. King

Tap dancing

King Oliver's Creole Jazz Band was one of
the first jazz bands.

their way to the Americas. For example, in **tap dancing,** you use your feet like drums. Tap dancing combines the rhythms and style of African dances with the footwork of English and Irish dances. The **Charleston** is another dance that experts believe is based on dances from Africa.

African dances also inspired the **samba.** Slaves brought an early version of this dance to the South American country of Brazil. Now the samba is popular all over the world.

Samba dancers in
Brazil

The
Charleston

7

Musical Intruments

If you like to listen to folk, bluegrass, or country music, you probably know what a **banjo** is. But did you know that the banjo comes from Africa? It is thought that the first banjos started showing up in North America more than 300 years ago. They were made by African slaves, who built new versions of instruments they had played in their homeland.

Africa is still home to other instruments that have become popular around the world. In parts of Nigeria and Ghana, people use drums that can imitate the sounds of local African languages. With these **talking drums,** people can send news from village to village.

Another popular West African instrument is the **shekere.** It is a gourd covered by netting

The banjo (right) is based on instruments like this one from Cameroon (above).

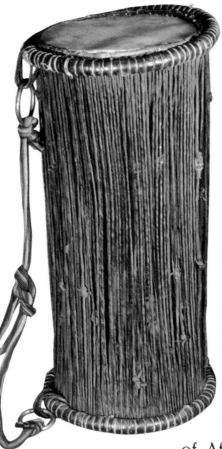

Nigerian talking drum

that has been strung with beads, seeds, or shells. It makes a wonderful rattling sound when you shake it.

The **mbira,** also called a **sansa** or **kalimba,** is a small keyboard instrument found throughout much of Africa. It is sometimes called a **thumb piano** because it sounds a little bit like a piano and you play it with your fingers and thumbs.

Thumb piano

Woman playing a shekere at an African-American festival

9

Coffee is one of the most popular beverages in the world. It is made from the seeds of the coffee tree, which comes from Africa. And speaking of beverages, do you enjoy cola? This refreshing beverage is made with **kola nuts,** which some experts believe were first brought to the Americas by African slaves.

Another food that originated in Africa is **sorghum.** Until the 1800s, the syrup that came from this plant was one of the most popular sweeteners in the United States.

Food

Kola nuts

Coffee

10

Kikuyu woman picking coffee beans in Kenya

Cola

Field of sorghum

Today, sorghum is used in other parts of the world to make bread and other foods. It is considered one of the world's most important food crops.

Okra

Okra

more food

Hopping John

Okra plant

Africans also brought **okra** overseas. This healthy vegetable is often used in a spicy kind of stew called **gumbo,** which was given its name by slaves. In fact, the word "gumbo" comes from an African word for "okra."

Have you ever tasted **hopping John?** This delicious dish is popular in the southern United States. Hopping John is made from **black-eyed peas,** known in Africa as cowpeas. Slaves introduced cowpeas to the United States.

Some experts also believe that the slaves brought **sesame seeds** with them from Africa. And many experts believe that slaves introduced **yams** to the Americas. Yams grow underground and are similar to sweet potatoes.

Sesame seeds

Black-eyed
peas

Man cooking gumbo
in Louisiana

Women selling yams and other vegetables in Mali

13

Animals

One of the most fascinating aspects of Africa is its incredible wildlife. Have you ever thought about how many animals you see at the zoo come from Africa?

The **African elephant** is the world's largest animal on land. It can weigh up to 16,000 pounds (7,300 kilograms). Another huge animal that comes from Africa is the **white rhinoceros,** which can weigh almost 8,000 pounds (3,600 kg).

Africa is also home to the **hippopotamus.** It spends lots of time in rivers, with only its eyes, ears, and nose above the surface of the water.

African elephants, Tanzania

Another animal found only in Africa is the **giraffe,** which can grow up to 18 feet (5.5 meters) tall. Its long neck helps it reach up to pull the leaves off trees.

River
hippopotamus
and calf
(above)

Masai
giraffe,
Tanzania

White rhinoceros,
South Africa

Chimpanzee, Tanzania

more animals

The **chimpanzee** is one of the smartest animals in the world. In fact, scientists say that chimpanzees and human beings are related. They both belong to a group of animals called primates.

Another important primate is the **gorilla.** Gorillas live deep in the forests of Africa. But because people keep cutting down the forests and hunting the gorillas for food, not very many of these amazing and intelligent animals are left.

Western lowland gorilla, Central Africa

Cheetah, South Africa

Male lion, Kenya

The **cheetah** is the world's fastest cat. For brief periods, it can run at a speed of 60 miles (96 kilometers) an hour. That's as fast as a speeding car!

The **lion** is often called the king of the jungle. Once, these great beasts lived in many parts of the world. Today, almost all of them are found in Africa.

Africa is also home to the **plains zebra,** a kind of wild horse that is famous for its stripes.

Burchell's zebras, Kenya

Fashion

American
girl
wearing cornrows

Many hairstyles come from Africa. For instance, African slaves introduced **cornrows** to the Americas. This style is still popular today in the United States and Africa, as well as in other parts of the world.

Africa is also the home of the **hair pick.** In ancient African cultures, these objects were more than just tools for combing hair. Carved from wood, ivory, or bone, they gave clues about a person's family, ethnic group, history, and wealth.

18

Plastic hair pick (left) and traditional African comb, Ivory Coast (right)

In the late 1960s, as Black Americans began expressing renewed pride in their African heritage, plastic versions of these combs became popular in the United States.

People all over the world like to wear African jewelry, such as **cowrie-shell necklaces.** Cowrie shells have an important place in African history. For thousands of years, they served as money!

Cowrie-shell necklace

Ashanti man wearing
a kente-cloth robe

more fashion

Many beautifully patterned fabrics come from Africa.
The designs and fabrics vary according to the ethnic group that
made them. Today, African fabrics are popular all over the world.
Perhaps the most famous of such fabrics is **kente cloth.**
This beautiful material is made by the Ashanti and Ewe peoples
of Ghana and Togo.
Historically, kente
was the cloth of
kings and was worn
as festive dress on
special occasions.
Today, many African-
Americans wear
kente cloth to
celebrate their African
heritage.

African fabrics

American boy wearing
a kente-cloth cap

African women
wearing boubous at a
celebration in Mali

Many African-style garments are popular
in the United States. Among these are the
dashiki, a tunic worn by men; and the
boubou, a loose-fitting garment worn by both
men and women. Both the dashiki and the
boubou come from West Africa.

American family wearing African-style
clothing, including dashikis
(father and sons)

21

Wooden mask of the Bena Biombo people, Congo

Wooden mask of the Chokwe culture, Angola

Art

People from all over the world collect artwork from Africa, and artists from other lands have learned a lot by copying African styles. For the African people, art is an important part of everyday life. Africans believe in bringing creativity and beauty to everything they touch.

For example, Africa is famous for its **masks.** These play an important role in many social and religious ceremonies. Some masks are used to honor dead ancestors or to communicate with spirits. Others are used in growing-up ceremonies, which prepare children for adulthood. Still others are used to help teach people lessons. Among the most famous kinds are wooden masks from West Africa and masks made with beads and shells from Central Africa.

Masked ceremony of the Dogon people, Mali

Beaded mask of the Kuba culture,
Zaire

Wooden mask,
Ivory Coast

more art

African artists also make lots of beautiful sculptures, such as the wooden **Akua-ba dolls** made by the Ashanti people. These dolls represent the Ashanti ideal of beauty.

Ashanti Akua-ba doll

The Ashanti people believe that carrying an Akua-ba doll will help a young girl to someday have beautiful, healthy babies.

Turkana man sleeping on a headrest, Kenya

Headrest of the Tsonga peoples, Mozambique

Wooden stool of the Bongo peoples, Sudan

Some amazing furniture also comes from Africa. The Turkana people of Kenya, for example, are well-known for their **wooden headrests.** These objects are used like pillows. Traditionally, many African ethnic groups have made beautiful **carved stools** to honor royalty or highly regarded village members.

Make a Game from Africa

Mancala

Mancala may be the oldest game in the world. Today, people all over Africa love to play it. You can make your own game board—and then play mancala with your friends!

You'll need:

- an egg carton
- scissors
- tape or a stapler
- 48 marbles, dried beans, pebbles, or pieces of uncooked macaroni

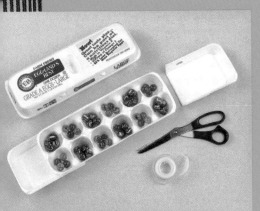

Making the mancala board

1. With an adult watching you, cut the lid off the egg carton.
2. Cut the lid of the egg carton in half crosswise.

3. Tape or staple one half of the lid to one end of the egg carton. Next, tape or staple the other half of the lid to the other end of the egg carton. This will create a tray at each end of the carton.

Setting up the game

Mancala takes two players. Place the board between you and your opponent. The egg-carton lids should be at each side, not facing you. Each of you takes twenty-four marbles and puts four into each of the six spaces in the row closest to you, so that one player has filled one long row with marbles and the other player has filled the other long row. The two larger trays on each end of the carton are called mancalas. Each of you gets the mancala to your right. Leave them empty at the start of the game.

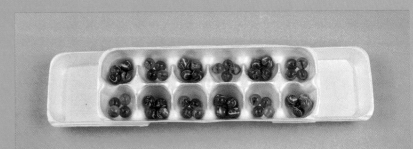

Throughout the game, you can move any of the marbles from your side of the board. You may not move the marbles on your opponent's side of the board.

Object of the game

The player with the most marbles in his or her mancala at the end of the game wins.

How the game is played

If you are the first player to go, scoop up all four marbles from any space on your side of the board. Now, moving counterclockwise, drop one marble into each bin that you come to. You'll drop the first marble in the first space to the right, the second marble in the second space to the right, and so on.

If you come to your mancala, drop a marble into it. If you have more marbles left after you drop one in the mancala, keep putting your remaining marbles into the bins on your opponent's side.

Sooner or later, you will come to your opponent's mancala. When you do so, skip over it. If your last marble lands in your mancala, you get to go again. Otherwise, it's your opponent's turn.

Capturing your opponent's marbles

If the last marble that you drop goes into an empty space on your side of the board, you get to capture any of your opponent's marbles in the space directly across from yours. When you capture these marbles, take all of them and put them in your mancala. Also put the marble that you used to do the capturing in your mancala. After you make a capture, it's the other player's turn.

How the game ends

The game ends when all six spaces in your row or all six spaces in your opponent's are empty. The player with marbles left on the board then puts those remaining marbles into his or her mancala. The player with the most marbles in their mancala at the end of the game wins.

Children in Kenya playing a version of mancala

How do you say....?

Africa has more than one thousand separate languages. Here's how you say "good morning" in a few of the many languages spoken in Africa:

language	where it's spoken	"good morning"	how to pronounce it
Arabic	parts of northern Africa	صباح الخير	sabaah al-khayr
Hausa	parts of Nigeria and Niger	Barka da kwana	bark-ah da quahn-a
Malagasy	Madagascar	Manao ahoana	ma-na-OH-na
Shona	Zimbabwe	Mangwanani	mang-wa-NA-nee
Swahili	Kenya, parts of East Africa	Habari ya asubuhi? (to a boy or man)	ha-BA-ree ya a-soo-BOO-hee
		Habari za asubuhi? (to a girl or woman)	ha-BA-ree za a-soo-BOO-hee
Tswana	Botswana, parts of South Africa	Dumela	DOO-mee-lah
Wolof	Senegal, parts of Gambia	Jama nga fanaan	JA-ma nga fa-NAHN
Xhosa	parts of South Africa	Molo	MAW-law
Yoruba	Nigeria	Ẹ káàárọ̀	eh ka-a-a-raw
Zulu	South Africa	Sawubona	sah-woo-BAW-nah

To find out more

Here are some other resources to help you learn more about Africa:

Books

Arnold, Caroline. **African Animals.** William Morrow & Company, 1997.

Ayo, Yvonne. **Eyewitness: Africa.** DK Publishing, 2000.

Bramwell, Martyn. **Africa** (The World in Maps). Lerner Publications, 2000.

Newman, Shirlee P. **The African Slave Trade.** Franklin Watts, 2000.

Petersen, David. **Africa** (True Books). Children's Press, 1998.

Stelzig, Christine, and Fiona Elliot. **Can You Spot the Leopard? African Masks.** Prestel USA, 1997.

Organizations and Online Sites

Africa Information Center
http://www.hmnet.com/africa/1 africa.html
Contains facts on all of the African countries. Includes maps.

African Voices
http://www.mnh.si.edu/africanvoices/
This Smithsonian Museum of Natural History site allows you to explore African objects and listen to Africans talk about their lives and culture.

Introduction to Africa
http://www.geographia.com/ indx06.htm
Explore several African countries and learn about the people, history, geography, and wildlife of the continent.

Living Africa
http://library.thinkquest.org/16645/ ?tqskip=1
This site—created by students and educators for Think Quest—includes games, quizzes, postcards, an atlas and photos of African people, places and animals.

National Museum of African Art
Smithsonian Institution
Education Department
950 Independence Avenue, SW
Washington, D.C. 20560-0708
http://www.si.edu/nmafa

PBS: Africa for Kids
http://pbskids.org/africa/
Read Swahili folk tales, make a mask, play thumb-piano tunes, and learn about other aspects of African culture.

Glossary

ancestor relative who lived in the past

ancient very old

civilization complex society with a stable food supply, division of labor, some form of government, and a highly developed culture

colony territory governed by a distant country

continent one of the great land masses of Earth

culture the beliefs and customs of a group of people that are passed down from generation to generation

enriched improved, added to in a positive way

ethnic group group of people whose members share the same culture, language, or customs

evidence fact or clue that helps prove that something is true

heritage something that is passed on from one's ancestors

ideal a standard of perfection, beauty, or excellence

inseparable impossible to separate

inspired influenced, spurred on

traditional handed down from generation to generation

30

Index

Look what doesn't come from Africa!

Some people think that just because lions come from Africa, **tigers** do too. But the truth is that tigers are from the continent of Asia.

Meet the Author
Miles Harvey is the author of several books for young people. He lives in Chicago with his wife, Rengin, and his children, Azize and Julian.

32